DK SUPERGUIDES

SWIMMING

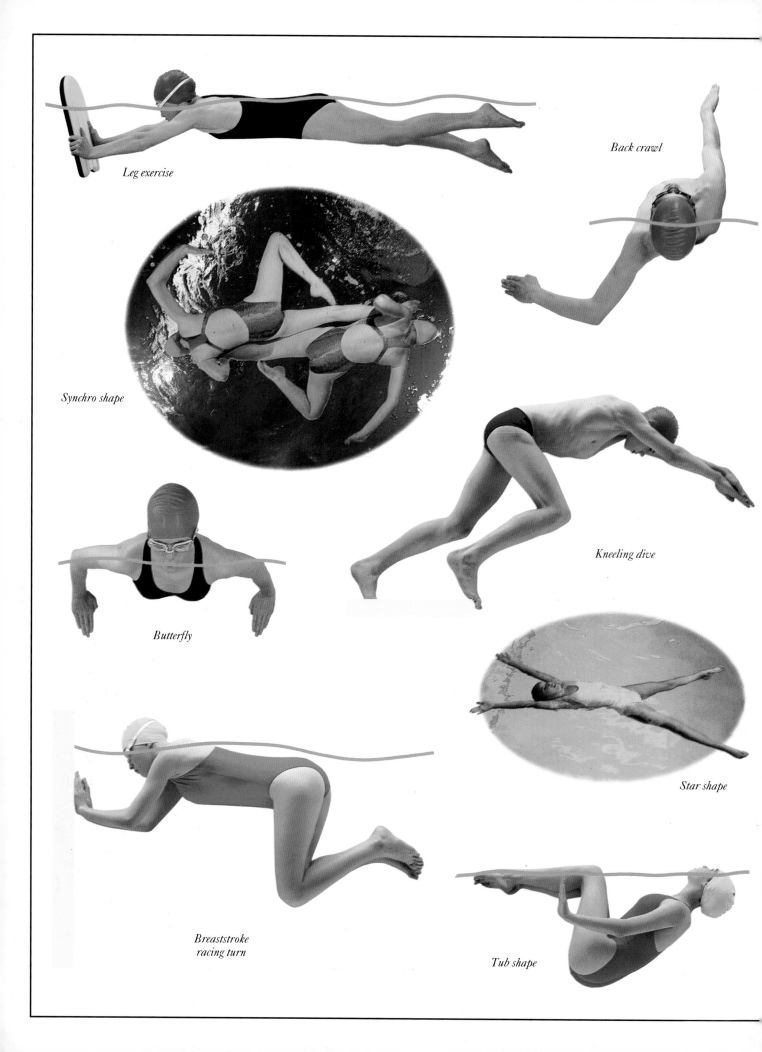

Leg exercise

Back crawl

Synchro shape

Kneeling dive

Butterfly

Star shape

*Breaststroke
racing turn*

Tub shape

Adjusting goggles

Ready to swim

DK SUPERGUIDES
SWIMMING

Written by Rick Cross
Foreword by Jeff Rouse

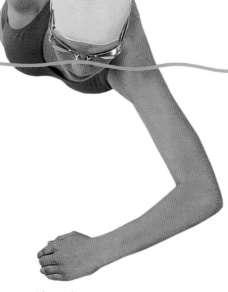

Alternating arms

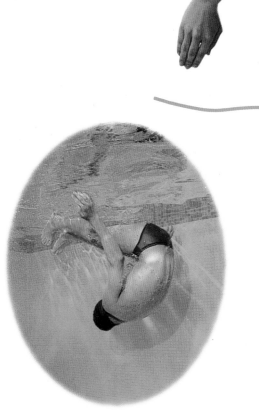

*Forward
somersault*

Front crawl

DORLING KINDERSLEY
London • New York • Sydney • Delhi

DK www.dk.com

A DORLING KINDERSLEY BOOK

DK www.dk.com

Project editor Lee Simmons   **Project art editor** Penny Lamprell
Editor Elinor Greenwood   **Art editor** Rebecca Johns
Photography James Jackson
DTP Designer Almudena Díaz
Picture researchers Mollie Gillard and Andrea Sadler
Production Josie Alabaster and Orla Creegan

The young swimmers

Harry Bond, Annabelle Halls, Marvin Jones, Jun King, Greta McLachlan,
Lisa Morrison, Laura Mulford, Kaya Ramjee, Melanie Stables

This revised edition published in Great Britain in 2000 by
Dorling Kindersley Limited
9 Henrietta Street, London WC2E 8PS
First published as *The Young Swimmer*, 1997

2 4 6 8 10 9 7 5 3

A CIP catalogue record for this book is available from the British Library.

ISBN 0 7513 2810 3

Colour reproduction by Colourscan, Singapore
Printed and bound in Italy by L.E.G.O.

Contents

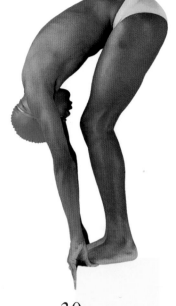

To all young swimmers

"Participation in the Olympics was always a dream of mine, so with a gold around my neck all I can say is 'thumbs up' to a dream come true!"

NO MATTER who you are or where you live, swimming is a rewarding activity to learn. This sport can provide you, as it did me, with the skills necessary to propel you through life; goal setting, time management, work ethic, and self-confidence are several of these important qualities. Swimming is a full-body exercise that provides you with excellent physical conditioning. But swimming is fun too, as anyone can tell you who has spent the afternoon floating, splashing, and playing in the pool. Confidence in the water can also lead to other endeavours such as water polo, water-skiing, and surfing. I hope that after reading this book you will appreciate how exciting and enriching swimming can be as a hobby, or a career.

Jeff Rouse

"The home stretch of any race never looks easy!"

"Believe it or not, I have a great time during workout!"

"The start of a race is my first opportunity to shine, so I make sure my form and focus are sharp!"

"After this great swim in Phoenix, USA in 1996, I knew I was one step closer to winning an Olympic gold medal."

History of swimming

ANCIENT CARVINGS found in the Middle East suggest that people have been able to swim for over 4,000 years. Swimming began as a survival skill, and only really became popular as a sport in the 19th century. Early strokes included the breaststroke, sidestroke, and various forms of front crawl. The butterfly was the most recent stroke to be invented. It was used in breaststroke races until 1952, when it became an event in its own right.

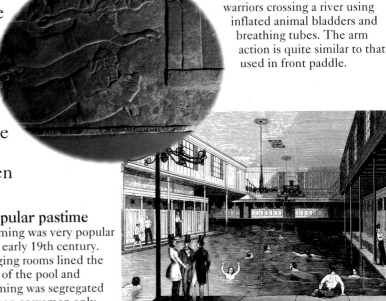

Swimming with pig bladders
This stone frieze from ancient Iraq, dating from 869 B.C., shows warriors crossing a river using inflated animal bladders and breathing tubes. The arm action is quite similar to that used in front paddle.

A popular pastime
Swimming was very popular in the early 19th century. Changing rooms lined the edges of the pool and swimming was segregated into men or women only.

Weissmuller went on to become a film star, starring as Tarzan.

Johnny Weissmuller
Weissmuller was one of the most famous American swimmers. In the 1928 Olympics he won nearly all the sprint titles. Because of improved methods of communication, his swimming actions were recorded, studied, and copied around the world.

Mark Spitz
At the 1972 Olympic Games in Munich, Germany, US swimmer Mark Spitz established himself as one of the greatest swimmers of all time. During the games he won seven individual events, all in world record time. He also swam in three team relay events.

Spitz at the 1972 Olympics. During his career he set 26 world records.

A man's typical bathing suit from 1921.

Printed stripes improve the flow of water over the body.

The close-fitting Acquablade legsuit is for men and women.

Costume design
Swimming costumes have come a long way since the beginning of the century. Then, costumes were made of wool and were cumbersome and heavy. Nowadays, advances in technology have resulted in fabrics that help to make swimmers more streamlined and drastically improve their speed.

Starting swimming

TO START OUT in swimming you only really need a swimming costume and a towel. However, if you plan to swim regularly with a club you will also need some of the items shown here. A track suit, or other warm clothing, pool shoes, a cap, and goggles are important. Later, your coach might suggest using equipment such as floats, kickboards, and pull buoys. Ask your coach about the sort of food you should eat. You should certainly consider using a drinking bottle if you start training sessions.

A cap makes you more streamlined in the water.

Swimmers wear swimsuits two sizes too small to streamline their bodies.

An extra towel may come in useful during training sessions or when attending swimming events.

Swimming costume
To cut down on drag in the water it is important that your swimming costume is the correct size and fits snugly. Most clubs have their own team outfit in the club's colours, which members can buy.

Joining a club
Join a club to get expert advice on how to improve your swimming skills and also get the opportunity to take part in club events. Inquire at your local pool or write to your nearest swimming association (see page 45) for information. Visit a club and watch the coaches at work to see what a training session involves.

Track suit

Wear your track suit to keep warm before and after training and also between swimming events at competitions. Your track suit should be loose and comfortable.

Caps make it easy to identify team members in the water.

A costume with a close-fitting, high neck will cut down on drag.

Keep a plastic drinks bottle handy in your sports bag.

Always change into pool shoes when at the pool, as outdoor shoes are unhygienic.

You can store clothing and other equipment in a sports bag.

Basic equipment

Your coach will help you decide what equipment you need.

Hand holds

Pull buoys

These two types of pull buoy are specially designed for arms-only work. They fit lengthways between your legs, just above your knees.

Floats and kickboards

Floats and kickboards are useful buoyancy aids for legs-only work. Floats will help you improve your technique if you are starting out. If you already swim, kickboards can help you strengthen your legs.

Paddles and mitts

Use hand paddles or hand mitts for extra arm-strengthening work. Make sure they are the correct size for your hands.

Hand mitts

Hand paddles

The flexible material enables you to change your hand shape.

Weighted dive rings

Dive for rings to practise swimming underwater with your eyes open.

Chamois towel

A chamois is very absorbent, drying you quickly and efficiently.

Nose clips stop water going up your nose.

Goggles

Goggles will protect your eyes from pool chemicals and will help you see more clearly in the water.

Tuck loose ends of elastic into headstrap.

1 To put goggles on safely, hold the eye pieces on your eyes with one hand and hold the strap with the other.

2 Stretch the strap over the back of your head and position it comfortably just above your ears.

Where to swim

SWIMMING IS THE perfect way to have fun and stay fit. All you need to do is find out where your local pool is. You can take swimming lessons here, or join a local club. Pools have changing rooms, lockers for clothes and valuables, showers, footbaths, and lifeguards. Many pools have sides higher than the water level. Others are called "deck level" because the water washes over the edges. Competition pools are usually 50 metres (164 ft) long with separate diving pits.

Open-water swimming

Open-water swimming and other water sports are very enjoyable, especially if you follow basic water safety rules (see pages 40-41). Make sure you are a strong swimmer, and don't go swimming alone. Learn the meaning of warning flags and buoys. Ask lifeguards for information about water conditions.

Outdoor pools

While many international venues are indoors, some countries with a warm climate have open-air pools. The 1991 European Championships, were held at this outdoor pool in Athens, Greece. Here, a training session for the event is in progress.

Lane markers

Lane markers are used to stop people from swimming into each other's paths. Some are called anti-wave markers because they have discs which stop waves, or backwash, from spreading into another swimmer's lane.

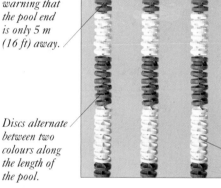

A third colour change is a warning that the pool end is only 5 m (16 ft) away.

Discs alternate between two colours along the length of the pool.

The plastic discs are threaded over a wire.

Competition pools

This picture shows Ponds Forge in Sheffield, England. As with some competition-size pools, it has movable booms at each end, so the length can be adjusted from 25 to 50 metres (82 to 164 ft). The pool also has an adjustable floor so that it can be used for a large variety of swimming competitions, water polo, or synchronized swimming.

Electronic scoreboard

Presentation podium

Electronic timing pads

False-start rope

Starting blocks

Movable booms

Anti-wave lane markers

Black lines on pool floor indicate centre of lanes.

5-m (16-ft) warning flags

Diving rules

1.8 m

Diving into the water head-first can be very dangerous, so it's important to follow certain rules.

• DO take notice of pool depth markers.

• DO go through the proper learning stages with your coach before diving.

• DO NOT attempt a racing dive in water less than 1.8 m (6 ft) deep.

Warning signs
Warning signs, such as flags and boards, can be seen posted by lifeguard patrol stations and along the beach. They mark out the areas you can or cannot swim in (see page 40).

Warming up/Cooling down
• Always allow sufficient time for both.

• Warming up before you swim should be both exercises on land and a water workout.

• Cooling down afterwards brings your heart rate back to normal and helps you recover.

Nutrition
A car can't run without the right fuel and neither can you!

• Eat well on the day of a competition to give your body energy.

• Eat soon after a competition to replace lost energy.

• Drinking fluid, such as water, is essential. Drink a little at a time, but often.

Back crawl flags
Flags strung across the pool 5 m (16 ft) from each end warn backstroke swimmers that the pool end is near.

50-metre pool

Spectator stands

Diving pits have a minimum depth of 3.5 or 5 m (11 or 16 ft), depending on the board heights.

Diving boards of different heights

Competition officials stand by the lanes and check the timing, finishing order, and whether finishes are legal.

Starting block
For safety reasons blocks are fixed to the poolside and the top is made of non-slip fibreglass. The top slopes down to the front to help swimmers launch off smoothly. Speakers are inserted into the blocks so that all the swimmers hear the starting signal at the same time.

Rails used for backstroke starts.

Leisure pools
Some pools are leisure or fun pools. These have features such as wave-making machines and long, spiralling slides or chutes. The chutes are made slippery by constant running water.

Basic know-how

You can cheat at the beginning, by gently sculling with your hands.

IF YOU ARE JUST starting out in swimming, practising these floating and gliding exercises will increase your confidence in the water. Start with the mushroom float before trying out different shapes such as the star float or horizontal float. Floating and making different shapes on your front or back will show you how the shape you make in the water affects your balance.

Horizontal float
Try to get your body as level as possible with the surface, with your head just resting in the water.

Star float
Stretch out on the surface as if you were lying on a clock face with your arms at about 10 o'clock and 2 o'clock and your feet at about 4 o'clock and 8 o'clock. If you find the float difficult, try it on your front first. Keep your head level with your body.

Mushroom float
This float is sometimes called a jellyfish float and is a good exercise to start with if you are trying to float for the first time. Take a deep breath, lower your face into the water, then tuck your legs in tightly and hug them close. After sinking a little, you will gradually rise to the surface.

Floating
When floating, breathe in and out very gently so that your lungs stay full of air and keep you afloat.

Push and glide on your front

Push and glide is a useful skill to learn as it encourages you to stretch out and find the most efficient body position for gliding.

Push and glide
These skills will help when you come to learn starts and turns.

Keep your head down.

1 Stand with your back to the wall. Place one foot firmly against it and bend your other leg slightly. Stretch out your arms, and hold on to the front of the float, with your thumbs on top.

2 Bounce gently off your standing leg and place both feet side by side on the pool wall.

3 Now push off vigorously, stretching both legs out behind you. Glide along the surface with your arms and legs outstretched and your face in the water.

Hands on top
Another way to hold the float is to put your hands over the leading edge and rest your arms lightly on the upper surface of the float.

From lying to standing

From your front

When you first glide on your front without a float, you may find it difficult to stand up afterwards. Remember the following points as you are about to leave your glide position.

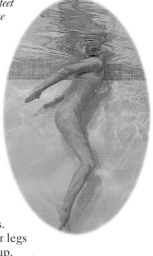

Plant your feet firmly on the bottom.

Exercising
Try this first when you are close to the pool wall.

1 Raise your head and press downwards and backwards with your hands at the same time. Your legs will then start to sink.

2 As your legs start to sink, bend your knees and bring them up towards your chest.

3 As your body rotates, your feet will begin to point downwards. Lower your legs and stand up.

From your back

Travelling backwards is less natural than travelling forwards, so you will find that standing up after gliding on your back is an important skill to learn. Start by gliding on your back.

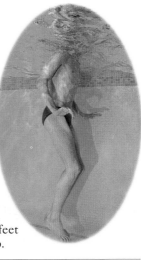

1 Drop your chin on to your chest and circle your hands backwards until they are level with your shoulders and close to the surface.

2 As your legs sink, bend your knees into your chest and scoop your hands towards your feet.

3 As you rotate, swing your knees under you, and point your feet downwards. Lower your feet and stand up.

Push and glide on your back

Practising push and glide on your back will help you to improve your backstroke start or turn.

Holding one float

Try this exercise with just one float, too. Hold the sides of the float and lay it flat along your thighs, at arm's length.

Standing up
If you want to stand up, it is easier if you let go of the floats and scoop your arms and hands as shown above.

Keep your hips up when gliding.

Keep your chin tucked in.

1 Stand facing the wall, holding a float under each arm. Bounce gently as you lean back to plant both feet firmly against the wall, just under the surface.

2 Push off strongly and straighten out both legs, stretching your body out. Try to keep the back of your head just resting in the water, with your ears at surface level.

Early skills

HAVING GAINED confidence in the water, you can try some more advanced activities. One of the most important swimming skills you can learn is sculling. All swimming strokes make use of sculling actions in some way. Just by changing the angle of your wrist you can travel head first, feet first, or even stay in one place. Sculling is also needed to perform other skills, such as treading water or somersaulting.

Stationary sculling

Sculling is a continuous action. Lie on your back and stretch out your hands, keeping your fingers together. Angle your palms out and down and, leading with your little finger, trace a figure-of-eight with your hands.

Your little finger always leads.

Your thumb starts and ends by your thigh.

Somersaults

Somersaults in the water help you become aware of where you are when upside-down, as well as being good fun! Knowing how to do somersaults will also help you when you start to do racing turns.

Forward somersault

When performing a forward somersault, it is easier to begin from a horizontal position on your front.

1 From your front, kick vigorously down with both legs together in a dolphin kick. At the same time, drop your chin on to your chest.

2 Begin to bend your knees and bring them forwards towards your chest.

3 As your knees come forwards, bend your arms and, turning your hands palms-up, push upwards. This will start you rotating into your somersault.

Tuck your knees in tightly.

4 While you are upside-down and still rotating, turn your palms to push towards your feet. This will help you to continue turning.

5 Remain in a curled-up position as you continue to turn. Your palms should continue to push towards your feet.

6 Continue pushing with your hands. As your head comes round to the surface, open out on to your front again.

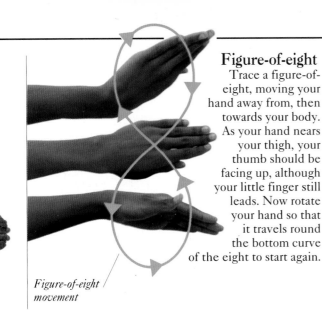

Figure-of-eight

Trace a figure-of-eight, moving your hand away from, then towards your body. As your hand nears your thigh, your thumb should be facing up, although your little finger still leads. Now rotate your hand so that it travels round the bottom curve of the eight to start again.

Figure-of-eight movement

Treading water

You will need to know how to tread water if you stop to rest in deep water, or if you need to gather your bearings in open water. Hold your arms out in front of you and scull with your hands, sweeping outwards and inwards.

Keep your hands close to the surface.

Your legs work in a gentle, vertical, breaststroke kick.

You can also try moving your legs as if you are riding a bicycle.

1 From lying in the water on your back, drop your head backwards into the water, bend your knees and begin to press your hands downwards and backwards.

Backward somersault

To prevent water going up your nose as you somersault backwards, slowly bubble air through your nose while you somersault. Alternatively, you can wear a nose clip.

Bring your knees to the surface.

6 Look for the surface, then begin to open out on to your back again.

2 To continue to rotate backwards, push down with your hands. Your feet will pass over your head.

Look for daylight above you.

Keep pushing your head backwards.

3 As you rotate, you will pass through a sitting position under the water. Press down with your palms and lift your hips towards the surface.

5 Scoop your hands down and back and continue to lift your knees.

4 Continue pressing down with your palms and lift your knees towards the surface.

On the move

TRY OUT SOME of the water confidence exercises shown here before you learn the main swimming strokes. Activities such as opening your eyes underwater, blowing bubbles, and breathing in and out as you lift your head in and out of the water will help you to become more familiar with the feel of the water.

Rolling

This simple rolling exercise will make you aware of a new way to move in the water. Take up a back-stretched glide position. Now, by using only the muscles in your back and abdomen, roll over on to your side, then on to your front, and finally return to your back.

Log roll

This exercise is sometimes called a log roll. Try to do one quickly without stopping. Can you turn in the opposite direction as well?

Surface dive

One way of submerging efficiently is to use a head-first surface dive. The advantage of this dive is that the first arm action can be part of a swimming stroke, usually breaststroke. You should not wear goggles when doing this dive.

1 From a swimming position, pull down with your hands and begin to bend at your hips. Breathe in just before you lower your head and pull down.

Keep your legs straight along the surface.

Begin to pike, or bend, at the waist.

Underwater games

To familiarize yourself with both breathing and seeing underwater, try these games with friends in the shallow part of the pool, away from any diving.

Swimming through legs

Take it in turns to practise swimming through a friend's legs. Try to avoid coming into contact with them.

Pulling faces

Practise opening your eyes underwater by seeing who can make the silliest face.

Practising your surface dive

Diving for hoops on the bottom of the pool is a good way of practising your surface dive. You could even form teams with other swimmers and have a relay competition.

Do not challenge others on how long you can stay underwater.

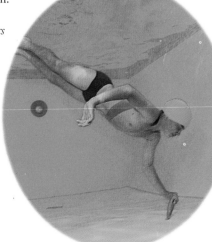

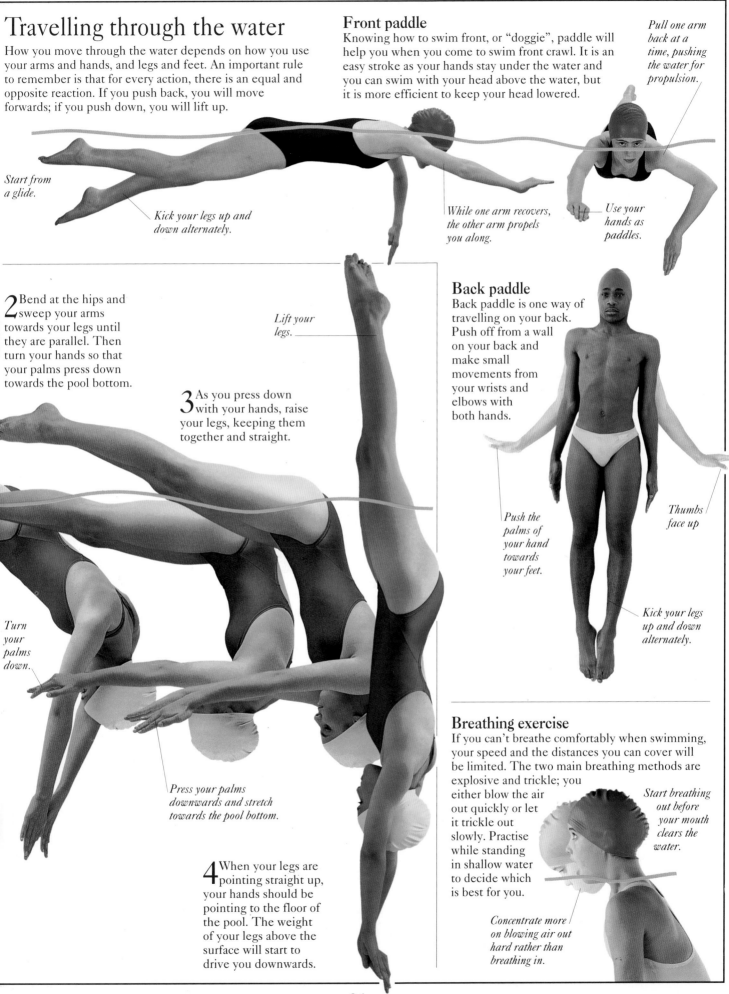

Travelling through the water

How you move through the water depends on how you use your arms and hands, and legs and feet. An important rule to remember is that for every action, there is an equal and opposite reaction. If you push back, you will move forwards; if you push down, you will lift up.

Start from a glide.

Kick your legs up and down alternately.

2 Bend at the hips and sweep your arms towards your legs until they are parallel. Then turn your hands so that your palms press down towards the pool bottom.

Lift your legs.

3 As you press down with your hands, raise your legs, keeping them together and straight.

Turn your palms down.

Press your palms downwards and stretch towards the pool bottom.

4 When your legs are pointing straight up, your hands should be pointing to the floor of the pool. The weight of your legs above the surface will start to drive you downwards.

Front paddle

Knowing how to swim front, or "doggie", paddle will help you when you come to swim front crawl. It is an easy stroke as your hands stay under the water and you can swim with your head above the water, but it is more efficient to keep your head lowered.

Pull one arm back at a time, pushing the water for propulsion.

While one arm recovers, the other arm propels you along.

Use your hands as paddles.

Back paddle

Back paddle is one way of travelling on your back. Push off from a wall on your back and make small movements from your wrists and elbows with both hands.

Push the palms of your hand towards your feet.

Thumbs face up

Kick your legs up and down alternately.

Breathing exercise

If you can't breathe comfortably when swimming, your speed and the distances you can cover will be limited. The two main breathing methods are explosive and trickle; you either blow the air out quickly or let it trickle out slowly. Practise while standing in shallow water to decide which is best for you.

Start breathing out before your mouth clears the water.

Concentrate more on blowing air out hard rather than breathing in.

Front crawl

FRONT CRAWL IS the fastest and most efficient of all the swimming strokes. To swim it correctly, your body must be as streamlined and horizontal as possible, and your legs and arms must move continuously. Each arm, in turn, propels you through the water. At the same time, your legs kick alternately up and down to keep you balanced. Your face stays in the water, even when you turn to breathe. There is no actual event called front crawl, but it is the most common choice of stroke in the freestyle event.

Arm position

Turn your face back into the water.

1 Turn your left hand so your thumb enters the water first, palm angled out and down. Your arm should be bent slightly and close to your body's centre line. Turn rather than lift your head to breathe.

2 Once your hand is in the water, push it backwards like a paddle, bending your elbow. Rolling slightly to your left will help you keep your hand close to the centre line.

When to breathe in

Michelle Smith, the Irish Olympic gold medallist, turns her head towards the arm leaving the water. She opens her mouth wide and takes a deep breath in behind the bow wave before turning her head back to face downwards.

How to breathe out

You can either use "trickle" breathing, gradually letting the air out whilst your face is still in the water, as shown here, or "explosive" breathing, when you blow the air out very hard just as you turn your head out of the water to breathe in.

Your heels should just break the surface.

Stretch out your legs.

Turn your toes in so that your feet brush past each other.

Your knees will bend slightly.

Co-ordination

Kick your legs up and down alternately at all times.

Keep your feet close to the water's surface.

1 As you stretch your left arm out in front of you, turn your head to the right, take a quick breath in, then turn your face back into the water. As your right hand exits, by your thigh, your body should roll to your left.

2 As your left hand sweeps down and back through the water, turn your palm to face your feet. As your right hand travels over the water your upper arm should pass close to your ear.

3 As your left hand moves back towards your thigh, reach your right hand forwards, ready for entry.

Alternate arms
Your right arm alternates with your left arm in exactly the same way.

Keep looking forwards and down.

3 As your left hand moves down and back towards your thigh, begin to straighten your elbow.

4 As your left arm straightens, brush your thumb past your thigh. Lift your left elbow so that it leaves the water first, before your hand. Turn your hand so that your little finger leads.

Leg strengthening
For this exercise, kick hard, up and down, starting the movement from your hips and finishing it with a whip-like action at your stretched ankles and feet.

Warming up
To increase the flexibility of your shoulders and spine, try this exercise. Place one hand over the back of the other, stretch your arms above your head, then gently bend from side to side, keeping your body straight.

5 As you raise your left elbow and hand clear of the water, roll your shoulders towards the hand entering the water.

Exercising
Always ask for your coach's advice before doing any exercises.

Keep your elbow high as your arm leaves the water.

Keep your face in the water at all times.

Streamlined body
Imagine a straight line running down the centre of your body, from your forehead to your feet. Try to keep your hands and feet as close as possible to this imaginary line at all times. Rolling your body towards the hand leaving the water will help. Turn your head just enough to allow you to breathe.

Your body will roll naturally towards the arm entering the water.

Breathe towards the arm leaving the water.

Keep your fingers close together.

Bend your elbow as you lift your arm.

Keep your shoulders level with your head.

4 As your left hand passes your thigh, it should be turned so that your little finger leads. Lift your left elbow so it leaves the water first, followed by your hand. Your right hand enters the water and starts to pull your body along.

5 As your left arm travels forwards, try to keep both hands close to the centre line. To do this, bend your elbows and roll your shoulders towards the hand entering the water.

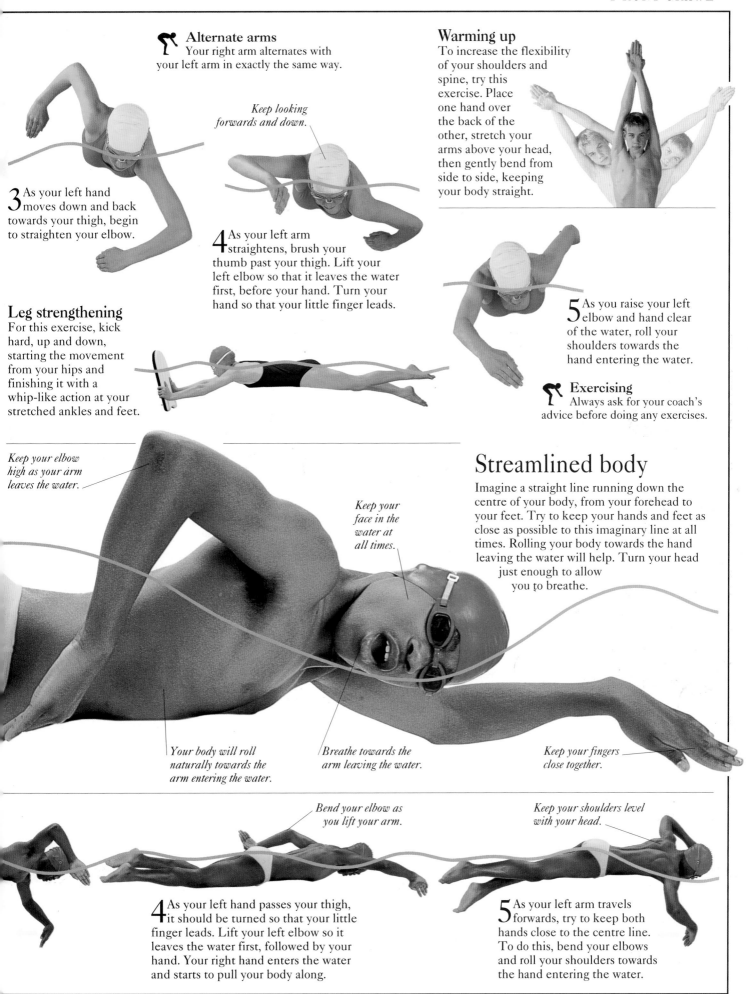

Back crawl

WHILE THE COMPETITIVE event is called backstroke, meaning any stroke swum on the back, the only stroke you will see being used in competitions is back crawl. It is not as fast as front crawl or butterfly, but it is still the fastest method of travelling on your back. You should aim for a streamlined body position, while inclining your body slightly to keep your kick under the water. Ensure that your arms and legs move continuously at all times.

Keep your head still throughout.

Focus on a line or mark on the ceiling to help you swim in a straight line.

Body roll
Practise rolling your body and shoulders towards your entering arm. This will place your entering hand into a better position for propulsion and your exiting hand into a better position for recovery.

Alternate arms
Your arms should work continuously, your right arm alternating with your left.

Streamlined
Here you can see Jeff Rouse swimming in the backstroke event at Phoenix, USA, 1996.

"My hips and body are rotating towards my arm that is about to enter the water. This rotation helps me keep my body in the most streamlined position possible."

Straighten your knees on the down kick.

Stretch your feet and ankles.

Bend your knees slightly on the upkick.

Your legs kick diagonally as your body rolls.

Intoeing
Your feet will make more efficient paddles if you turn them inwards, so that your big toes brush past each other.

Breathing
Practise breathing in as one arm recovers and out as the other arm recovers.

Co-ordination

Right arm is in recovery.

Arm remains straight until catch point.

Hand at catch point.

1 This sequence explains the efficient bent arm, or "S" pull. Keep your left arm in line with your shoulder as your left hand enters the water. Your little finger leads, palm facing out and arm fully stretched. Your right arm should be about to exit.

2 Once your left hand is in the water, turn your palm to face down and stretch your hand forwards, down, and out to catch point, 15-20 cm (6-8 in) below the surface. Roll your body towards your left arm as your right arm begins its recovery over the water.

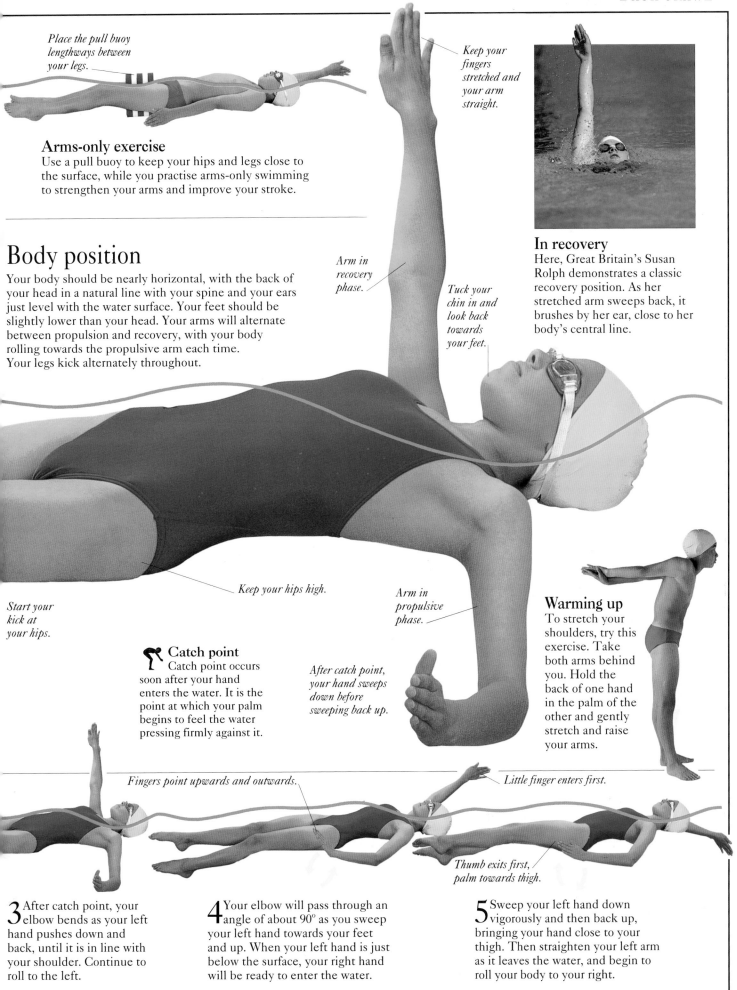

Place the pull buoy lengthways between your legs.

Arms-only exercise
Use a pull buoy to keep your hips and legs close to the surface, while you practise arms-only swimming to strengthen your arms and improve your stroke.

Keep your fingers stretched and your arm straight.

Arm in recovery phase.

Tuck your chin in and look back towards your feet.

In recovery
Here, Great Britain's Susan Rolph demonstrates a classic recovery position. As her stretched arm sweeps back, it brushes by her ear, close to her body's central line.

Body position
Your body should be nearly horizontal, with the back of your head in a natural line with your spine and your ears just level with the water surface. Your feet should be slightly lower than your head. Your arms will alternate between propulsion and recovery, with your body rolling towards the propulsive arm each time. Your legs kick alternately throughout.

Keep your hips high.

Start your kick at your hips.

Arm in propulsive phase.

Catch point
Catch point occurs soon after your hand enters the water. It is the point at which your palm begins to feel the water pressing firmly against it.

After catch point, your hand sweeps down before sweeping back up.

Warming up
To stretch your shoulders, try this exercise. Take both arms behind you. Hold the back of one hand in the palm of the other and gently stretch and raise your arms.

Fingers point upwards and outwards.

Little finger enters first.

Thumb exits first, palm towards thigh.

3 After catch point, your elbow bends as your left hand pushes down and back, until it is in line with your shoulder. Continue to roll to the left.

4 Your elbow will pass through an angle of about 90° as you sweep your left hand towards your feet and up. When your left hand is just below the surface, your right hand will be ready to enter the water.

5 Sweep your left hand down vigorously and then back up, bringing your hand close to your thigh. Then straighten your left arm as it leaves the water, and begin to roll your body to your right.

Breaststroke

IN BREASTSTROKE, your arms and legs stay under the surface all the time. This means you have more water resistance to overcome and is the main reason why breaststroke is the slowest of the four strokes. It is an easy, enjoyable stroke to learn, as you can raise your head above the surface to breathe. Practise the leg kick while holding a float, before adding the arm actions.

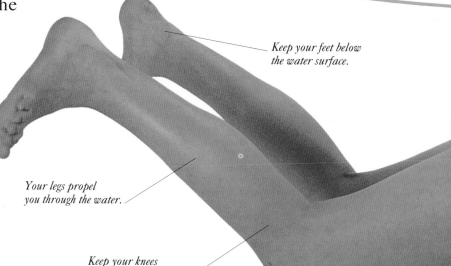

Exercising
Try to spread your knees just wider than hip width as you drive your legs round and back. This way, your legs will recover faster and will be ready to give you more propulsion sooner.

Keep your feet below the water surface.

Your legs propel you through the water.

Keep your knees well behind your hips.

Co-ordination

Keep your body streamlined.

1 Start from a good, fully stretched push-and-glide position with your ears squeezed between your arms. Try to get into this position between each full stroke. Your coach might advise you to reduce this glide as your swimming improves.

2 From the glide, sweep your hands outwards to a point just wider than shoulder width, then turn your palms down. This point is known as catch point. The rest of your body remains in the same position as before.

Hands at catch point.

Point your toes backwards.

Breaststroke competition
Here, swimmers can be seen using the "high-lift" style in the women's breaststroke event at the International Swimming Cup in 1990. Nowadays, many swimmers use this style to improve their speed.

Turn your feet out.

Keep your hips and shoulders horizontal.

Pull your toes towards your shins.

The whip kick
The whip kick helps you get the most out of the powerful thrust of your legs. After bringing your heels up close to your bottom, with your knees about hip-width apart, turn your feet up and out and kick vigorously round and back.

Body position

To swim breaststroke well, angle your body from your shoulders, so your feet stay under the surface. As you push your legs back and round, your arms should be stretching forwards, with your head almost under the surface.

Keep your head in a streamlined position.

Breathe in as your hands come beneath your chin.

Stretch your arms forwards as far as you can after breathing.

Incline your body downwards slightly.

Keep your hips just below the surface.

The high-lift style

Here, Krisztina Egerszegy of Hungary swims breaststroke by lifting her upper body out of the water and moving her hips up and down in a wave-like action. This reduces water resistance, helping her swim faster.

Bring your heels towards your bottom.

Breathe in as your head and shoulders rise.

Drop your hips.

Drive your legs round and back.

3 After catch point, bend your elbows sharply so that your palms sweep round, down, and back. Gradually start lifting your head and shoulders forwards and up and begin to bend your knees.

4 Continue to bend your elbows and circle your hands. After they pass below your elbows, begin to bring them up towards your chin. Turn your feet up and out, ready to drive back.

5 Stretch your arms forwards, and return to the original glide position, lowering your head back so you are streamlined once again.

After catch point

Once your hands have reached catch point, they begin the propulsive stage. Press your hands out, down, and back as you begin to bend your arms.

Arm action

In order to improve your propulsion through the water keep your shoulders horizontal and your elbows high. Sweep your hands back and in towards your chest, pushing against the water as you do so.

Thigh and ankle warm-up

Supporting yourself against a wall, hold your foot and slowly and gently pull it back to your thigh.

Butterfly

BUTTERFLY WAS INVENTED in the early 1930s but was swum as a version of breaststroke until 1952, when it was officially recognized as a new stroke. Originally the kick was similar to that used in breaststroke, but now the more efficient up-and-down "dolphin kick" is used. Because your arms recover over the water and your legs and body undulate there is far less resistance and more propulsion than in breaststroke.

Arm position

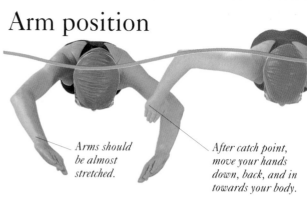

Arms should be almost stretched.

After catch point, move your hands down, back, and in towards your body.

1 Your hands enter the water about shoulder-width apart, thumbs first and palms angled outwards. Your face should be in the water.

2 After entry, sweep your hands outwards to catch point, wide of your shoulders, then bend your elbows.

Co-ordination

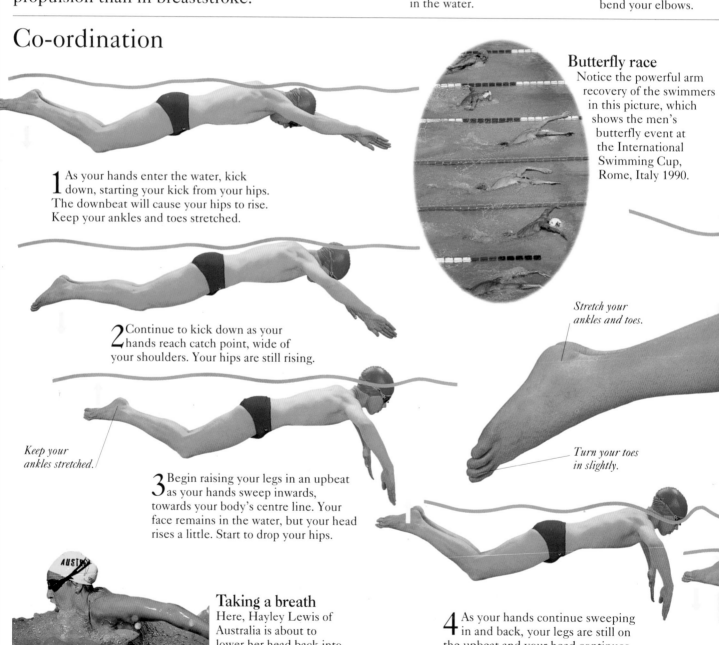

1 As your hands enter the water, kick down, starting your kick from your hips. The downbeat will cause your hips to rise. Keep your ankles and toes stretched.

2 Continue to kick down as your hands reach catch point, wide of your shoulders. Your hips are still rising.

Keep your ankles stretched.

3 Begin raising your legs in an upbeat as your hands sweep inwards, towards your body's centre line. Your face remains in the water, but your head rises a little. Start to drop your hips.

Taking a breath
Here, Hayley Lewis of Australia is about to lower her head back into the water after breathing, but before her arms finish their recovery.

Butterfly race
Notice the powerful arm recovery of the swimmers in this picture, which shows the men's butterfly event at the International Swimming Cup, Rome, Italy 1990.

Stretch your ankles and toes.

Turn your toes in slightly.

4 As your hands continue sweeping in and back, your legs are still on the upbeat and your head continues to rise. Your hips continue to drop.

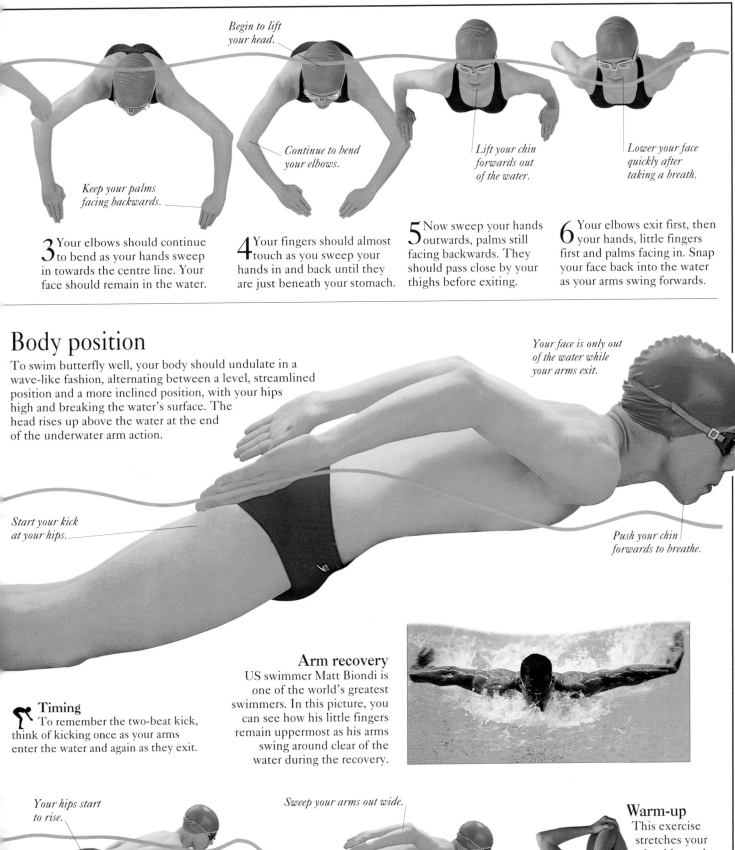

Begin to lift your head.

Continue to bend your elbows.

Lift your chin forwards out of the water.

Lower your face quickly after taking a breath.

Keep your palms facing backwards.

3 Your elbows should continue to bend as your hands sweep in towards the centre line. Your face should remain in the water.

4 Your fingers should almost touch as you sweep your hands in and back until they are just beneath your stomach.

5 Now sweep your hands outwards, palms still facing backwards. They should pass close by your thighs before exiting.

6 Your elbows exit first, then your hands, little fingers first and palms facing in. Snap your face back into the water as your arms swing forwards.

Body position

To swim butterfly well, your body should undulate in a wave-like fashion, alternating between a level, streamlined position and a more inclined position, with your hips high and breaking the water's surface. The head rises up above the water at the end of the underwater arm action.

Your face is only out of the water while your arms exit.

Start your kick at your hips.

Push your chin forwards to breathe.

Timing
To remember the two-beat kick, think of kicking once as your arms enter the water and again as they exit.

Arm recovery
US swimmer Matt Biondi is one of the world's greatest swimmers. In this picture, you can see how his little fingers remain uppermost as his arms swing around clear of the water during the recovery.

Your hips start to rise.

Sweep your arms out wide.

Warm-up
This exercise stretches your shoulder and upper arm. Gently pull your elbow across and down your back. Repeat with the other arm.

5 As your hands sweep outwards past your thighs, ready to exit, your legs start to move back down through the water.

6 As your arms recover over the water, your legs finish their downbeat and start rising again and your hips begin to drop.

Racing starts

MAKING A good start in competitions is vital, especially for short swimming distances. You need to get away from the starting block quickly and accurately judge your flight distance and the angle of entry into the water.

Kneeling dive

A kneeling dive is a good dive to learn first. Position yourself carefully so that you don't slip as you push off. Grip the pool edge with the toes of your front foot. You should travel both up and outwards.

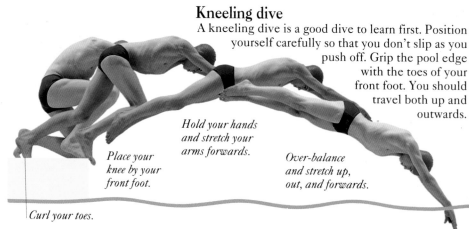

Hold your hands and stretch your arms forwards.

Place your knee by your front foot.

Over-balance and stretch up, out, and forwards.

Curl your toes.

Grab start

The grab start is the most common start for freestyle, breaststroke, and butterfly races, as it helps you get away from the block quickly.

1 At the command "Take your marks", bend down and hold on to the front of the block. Keep your hips above your knees.

2 On the word "Go!" pull sharply on the block. As you over-balance, push off hard with your legs to gain height and distance.

3 At the top of your flight, pike, or bend at the waist. Make sure your head is down as you go into the pike.

1.8 m

Bend your knees slightly.

Drive hard from the block.

Keep arms and legs fully stretched.

Grip the edge firmly with your toes.

Hand positions

You can either hold the edge of the block with your hands between your feet or just outside them.

Laws
Ask your coach to explain the competition laws on racing starts.

Other starts

Wind-up start

Wind-up starts are used in relay takeovers because you judge your take off by the speed of the incoming swimmer. Make a big circular movement up and back with your arms, then drive off powerfully with your legs.

Track start

This start gives a bigger push off. Grip the block with your hands and toes and put your weight on your back foot. Next, pull hard with your arms and push with your feet.

Transition

Front crawl

The transition is the time you are underwater, between entry and the first arm stroke. Make use of a powerful dive by continuing to stretch.

1 After entry, hold your stretched and streamlined position and flatten out. Then begin to stretch upwards in a glide. You will still be travelling at speed.

Keep your body stretched and streamlined.

1.8 m

Breaststroke

Your underwater arm pull in breaststroke is very strong, so the transition is deeper and longer than in front crawl.

1 Your entry should be slightly steeper than front crawl. After entry, flatten out into a glide.

Keep your stretched, streamlined position.

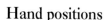

30

Back crawl start

Swing your arms past your head.

Stretch out your arms by your ears.

2 On the starting signal, throw your head up and back. At the same time swing your arms up and out and push off hard with your legs.

3 Stretch out, arch your back, and reach towards the water with your fingers. Your fingers should enter the water first.

1 Hold the rail and bring your feet up high. Bend your arms and pull your chin to the rail.

Back crawl start

The back crawl start begins in the water and is really a backward dive. Face the wall and hold on to the start rail, feet close to the surface. On the word "Go!", push off, stretching up and outwards. Do a few kicks underwater before surfacing to start your arm action. For safety always look behind you before you practise this move.

4 Open out from the pike by raising your legs. Stretch forwards and downwards towards your entry point.

1996 Olympics

This picture shows the start of a back stroke event. Each swimmer's flight is perfectly streamlined as they reach backwards towards entry.

The fully stretched and streamlined position for entry.

5 As you enter the water, continue to stretch forwards and downwards. Your hands enter the water first followed by your body, which passes through the "hole" in the water that your hands have made. The impact of the water will be considerable, so keep fully stretched.

⚠ **Safety**
Make sure the water is at least 1.8 m (6 ft) deep when you practise head-first entries. Check with a lifeguard, coach, or parent before diving.

Your entry should be as stretched and streamlined as possible.

2 Just as you begin to slow down, use your legs to drive you up to the surface.

3 Begin your first arm action just before you break the surface. Delay breathing for a couple of strokes.

The angle you enter the water will affect your transition into a stroke.

Start your leg action before your arm action.

Start your stroke as soon as possible.

Butterfly transition

2 As you begin to slow down, make a powerful double arm pull out, round and back to your hips. Follow this with a short glide.

Hold the glide position.

3 After the glide, keep your hands close to your chest as you move them forwards in recovery, ready for the first stroke on the surface.

This is similar to breaststroke, except it is shorter and shallower. You use a dolphin kick followed by a powerful double arm pull to bring you to the surface.

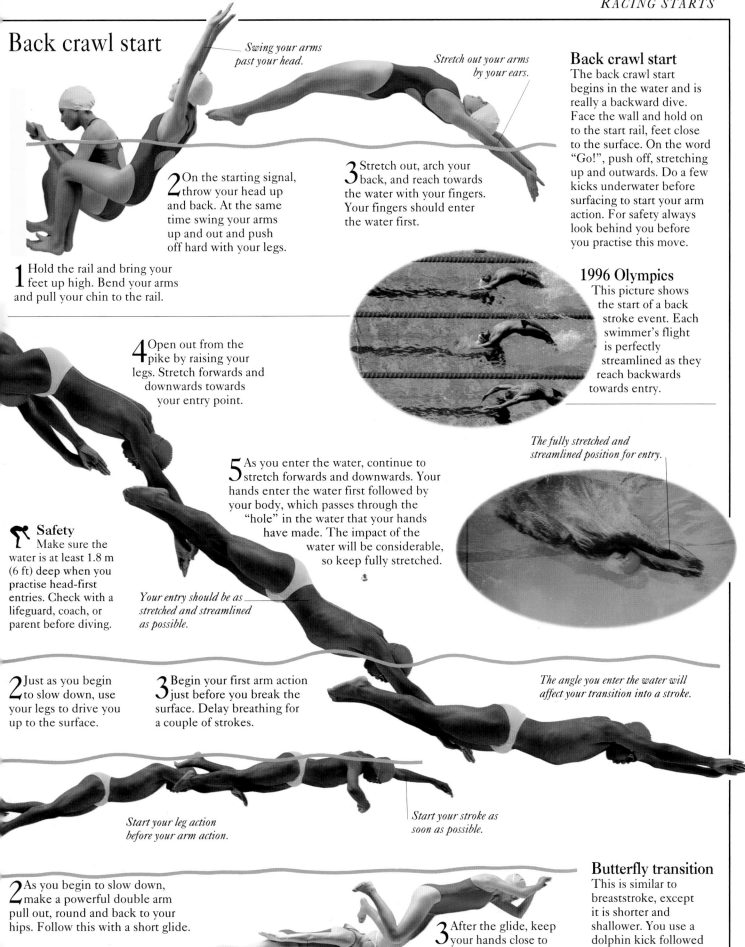

Racing turns

GOOD TURNS CAN save you valuable time during a race. Make use of your swimming speed as you approach the wall so that you can rotate quickly before planting your feet for a powerful push off. Front and back crawl turns include a somersault, while breaststroke and butterfly turns require more of a twisting movement and your hands touch the wall as well as your feet. Crawl turns are often called "tumble" turns, and the breaststroke and butterfly turns are sometimes called "touch" turns. Good turns only come through a lot of practice and hard work.

Back crawl turn

Back crawl and front crawl turns are very similar. Use the 5-m (16-ft) warning flags overhead as a guide to when to start your turn.

Bring your recovering arm out of the water and across your body's centre line.

Roll over.

Bring your leading hand back to your thigh.

Glide underwater, making use of the push.

Tuck your chin in and flip your legs over.

Push off forcefully on your back.

Plant your feet on the wall and stretch your arms forwards.

Front crawl turn

It is most important that you carry out the whole turn as smoothly as possible. The timing of the exact moment you need to start your turn will come from trying out different distances from the wall. To begin with, try starting the somersault at about 1–1.5 m (3–4 ½ ft) from the wall, then adjust it according to your results.

The push off

To get the most out of your turns, practise the push offs on their own, then you can add them to the turn.

Approach the wall at normal speed.

Keep your legs close together and parallel to the water surface.

Tuck your knees in to speed up your somersault.

1 At 1–1.5 m (3–4 ½ ft) from the wall, leave your trailing hand by your thigh and pull your leading hand back so that it is also by your thigh.

2 Turn your palms to face the pool bottom. To start the somersault, press your hands downwards, drop your chin towards your chest, and do a dolphin kick with your legs.

3 Flip your feet out of and over the water. You should be face-up under the water, with your hands beginning to move forwards towards your head.

Tumble turns

It is vital that competition swimmers know how to do fast, efficient turns.

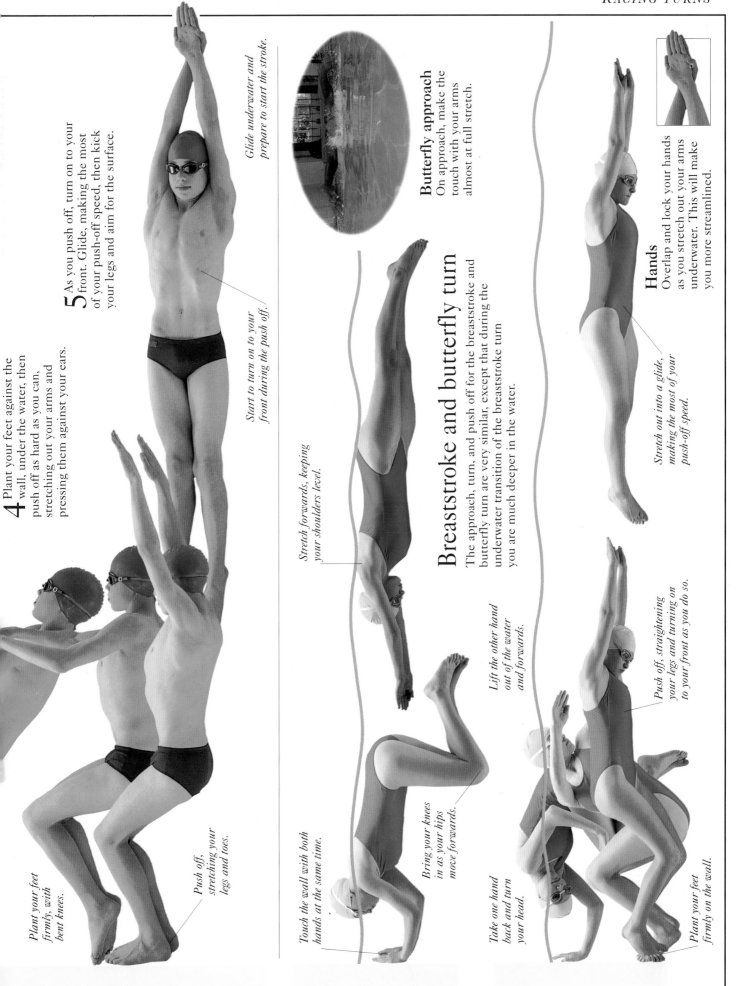

4 Plant your feet against the wall, under the water, then push off as hard as you can, stretching out your arms and pressing them against your ears.

5 As you push off, turn on to your front. Glide, making the most of your push-off speed, then kick your legs and aim for the surface.

Glide underwater and prepare to start the stroke.

Start to turn on to your front during the push off.

Plant your feet firmly, with bent knees.

Push off, stretching your legs and toes.

Butterfly approach
On approach, make the touch with your arms almost at full stretch.

Hands
Overlap and lock your hands as you stretch out your arms underwater. This will make you more streamlined.

Stretch out into a glide, making the most of your push-off speed.

Breaststroke and butterfly turn

The approach, turn, and push off for the breaststroke and butterfly turn are very similar, except that during the underwater transition of the breaststroke turn you are much deeper in the water.

Stretch forwards, keeping your shoulders level.

Touch the wall with both hands at the same time.

Bring your knees in as your hips move forwards.

Lift the other hand out of the water and forwards.

Take one hand back and turn your head.

Push off, straightening your legs and turning on to your front as you do so.

Plant your feet firmly on the wall.

33

Synchronized swimming

IF YOU LIKE swimming, gymnastics, and working to music then synchronized swimming is the sport for you. If you learn the basic sculls first, you can progress on to making different shapes in the water, which are called figures. In time, you will be able to combine the strokes, sculls, and figures and put them to expressive music.

Sculling practice

Locking ankles

Once you have mastered basic sculling, you can work with a partner. Link feet with your partner, squeezing your legs together. One partner performs a torpedo scull while the other performs a standard scull with their arms at their sides.

Using bottles

Buoyant plastic bottles will help keep you afloat while learning how to make different shapes with your body. Practise the flamingo position, shown here. Try to keep the extended leg straight.

Sculling

Sculling is a very important skill to learn. The movement starts from the shoulder. Sweep the palms of your hands away from your sides, little finger leading, and towards your sides, thumb uppermost. Try to keep your wrists firm, arms straight, and the movement continuous.

Point your fingers down, flexing from the wrist.

Reverse scull

Keep your hands in line with your forearm.

Flat scull

Point your fingers up. Keep your arms close to your body.

Standard scull

Canoe scull

To travel head first, lie on your front, with your body arched, your hips low, and your chin and feet at the surface. Stretch out your arms, keeping them close to your hips, and use a standard sculling action.

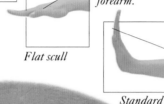

Point your fingers downwards.

Torpedo scull

To travel feet first, lie on your back with your legs together, your stomach in, and your hands above your head, shoulder-width apart. Press your arms and hands down into the water and use a standard scull, fingers pointing down.

Figures

A figure is a series of movements. All figures have different names, such as "oyster" and "tub". Once you have mastered good sculling techniques, you can combine these skills to make a sequence of shapes with your body, creating figures.

Oyster

1 Start with a flat scull on your back. Keep your head, hips, and feet at the surface. Keep your hands close to your hips and your toes pointed.

2 Lift your feet and drop your hips. Keep your body straight. Press your hands down and swing them around, behind your head.

Keep your arms and legs straight.

3 Lift your legs up and circle your arms around to touch your ankles.

Hold the oyster position until you are fully underwater.

Tub

Extend your head back in the water.

Keep your knees above your hips.

1 Do a flat scull on your back. Make sure your head, hips, and feet are at the surface, and scull evenly with your hands close to your hips.

2 Drop your hips down as you bend your knees and bring your lower legs up parallel to the water's surface. Turning towards your left shoulder, complete a full circle by doing a standard scull with your right hand and a reverse scull with your left hand.

Turn the tub figure by sculling with your hands.

Formations

As a synchronized swimmer, you can perform alone, with a partner, or in a group. This gives you the opportunity to make many different kinds of formation. You can use formations both on the water's surface and underwater. It is vital that you have mastered the basic skills before performing formations with other people.

Side bent knee link

Scull next to your partner, head to toe. Link together by holding each other's ankles close to your shoulders. Bend your outside leg, as shown here and point your toes so that your big toe touches your straight leg. Now do a standard scull with your outside arm to turn head-first or a reverse scull to turn feet-first.

Dolphin chain

This formation is performed underwater. Hold your partner's feet with one or two hands. Make sure you keep your body firm, your back arched, and your legs squeezed together. To turn the rotation, scull with one hand while you hold on with the other.

Open side bent knee link

Start with a side bent knee link. Roll on to your side to face outwards and extend and straighten your inside arm. To turn the formation do a standard scull. You can either keep your heads above or below the water.

Flat sculling will help you hold the cartwheel formation.

Squeeze your bottom muscles to keep your body arched underwater.

A nose clip will stop water going up your nose when underwater.

🏊 **On the surface**
A dolphin chain can be performed at the water's surface, too.

Keep your body straight.

Cartwheel

When doing formations in a group, you can make numerous shapes. To make a cartwheel, form a circle. Everyone's left leg should be touching in the middle of the circle. Each person bends their right leg and places it on the hip of the person to the right.

Point your toes

Ballet leg

Practise this position with bottles before you try sculling.

1 Do a flat scull on your back. Keep your hips and feet close to the surface. Extend your head, but keep your face above the surface.

2 Draw one leg up along your opposite thigh until your bent thigh is at right angles to your body. Keep the opposite leg straight.

3 Straighten the bent leg and bring it out of the water to make the ballet leg movement. Keep your body and other leg horizontal.

Events and competitions

AS A COMPETITIVE sport, swimming has a very strong following, from swimming clubs through to district, national, and international championships, culminating in the four-yearly Olympic Games. Swimming at the Olympics is part of the aquatics programme, along with synchronized swimming, water polo, and diving. The international rules are governed by the Fédération Internationale de Natation Amateur (FINA), which has over 160 member countries.

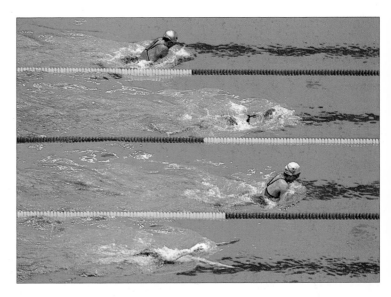

Triathlon
A newly created Olympic sport, the triathlon consists of three stages – swimming, cycling, and running. The Olympic distances are a 1.5-km swim, a 40-km bike ride, and a 10-km run. There are no stops between the three legs. Hundreds of competitors can enter a triathlon, and the races often start with a splash, like in this picture.

Individual medley race
A swimmer needs to excel in all four strokes to be successful in the individual medley. Competitors must swim an equal distance of each stroke in the order of butterfly, backstroke, breaststroke, and freestyle. The length of the leg is determined by the competition.

Heats and finals
Heats are swum if there are too many competitors in an event. The winners swim in the final. The fastest has the middle lane, the second and third fastest have lanes on either side, and so on, resulting in the familiar arrowhead, or "V" shape.

Relay races
There are two types of relay event – the freestyle relay and the medley relay. Each "leg" of the race is completed when the swimmer in the water touches the pool end. The medley relay must be swum in the following order: backstroke, breaststroke, butterfly, and freestyle.

The outgoing swimmer must be ready to leave the block the instant the touch is made.

Swimmers move from stroke to stroke without getting out of the water.

Proud winners of club medals.

Swimming for gold

As a member of a swimming club, you will get the chance to take part in club championships, then perhaps interclub competitions. Eventually you might compete at national level. All international swimmers start out as, and remain, club swimmers.

The Paralympics

The Paralympics are held every four years, and take place in the same country as the Olympics. Swimming is one of the top sports in the Paralympic Games. The swimmers are grouped together according to the level of their disability. International swimming rules are followed with only a few exceptions, such as the use of signals alerting blind swimmers of an upcoming turn or relay.

An Olympic win

The Olympic swimming programme comprises men and women competing in 16 events each. There are four different strokes across a range of distances and each race has a maximum of eight swimmers. There are preliminary heats, then the fastest swimmers go through to the semifinals, and then the finals. There is no greater thrill or reward for a swimmer than winning an Olympic gold. Here, world-record holder, Kieren Perkins of Australia is elated after winning the 1500-m freestyle event at the Atlanta Olympics in 1996.

Beth Botsford shows off her gold medal in the backstroke event at the Atlanta Olympics.

The Olympic Games

Olympic swimming has come a long way from the first modern Olympic Games held in Athens in 1896. Then the event began with swimmers dropped off in the Mediterranean having to swim back to shore. Swimmers nowadays enjoy hi tech pools, with temperature control and lane markers designed to reduce turbulence. Swimming has a status as one of the Games' glamour events and is one of the most popular spectator sports.

Taking it further

ONCE YOU CAN SWIM, a host of other new sports are opened up to you. Water sports are exciting, challenging, and varied. A water sport can be a hobby, a competitive sport, or even become a way of life. Whether you get your thrills from riding a wave, launching yourself off a high board, or playing fast-paced team games, there is something for all water-lovers. Water polo and diving can often be learnt in your local pool as part of the swimming programme. Windsurfing, surfing, and water-skiing have their own clubs and associations and operate on amateur and professional levels.

An elegant back dive.

Diving

This is a very demanding sport, requiring considerable practice and dedication. It combines the skills of a gymnast and trampolinist with the grace and poise of a dancer. It became an Olympic sport in 1904 and since then has, literally, changed in leaps and bounds. There are competitions for both men and women, and there are two disciplines: springboard, at 1 m and 3 m, and high (firm) board at 10 m. Depth of water is very important and you should check with your local pool to find out if it is safe to learn there.

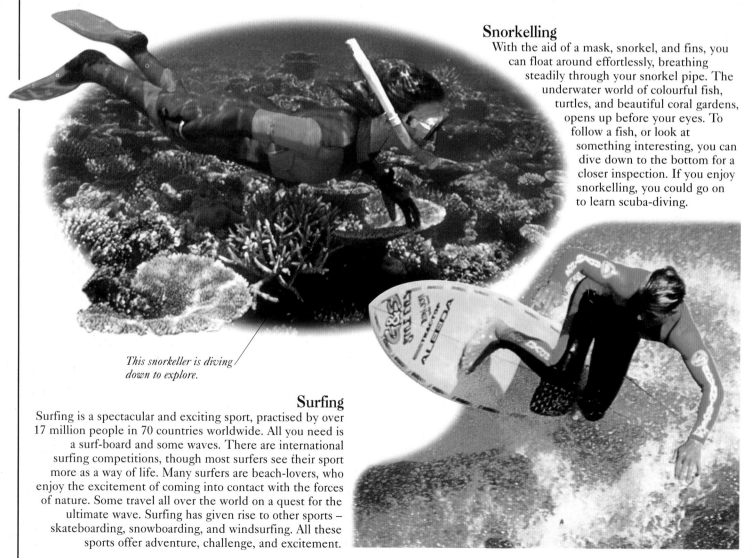

Snorkelling

With the aid of a mask, snorkel, and fins, you can float around effortlessly, breathing steadily through your snorkel pipe. The underwater world of colourful fish, turtles, and beautiful coral gardens, opens up before your eyes. To follow a fish, or look at something interesting, you can dive down to the bottom for a closer inspection. If you enjoy snorkelling, you could go on to learn scuba-diving.

This snorkeller is diving down to explore.

Surfing

Surfing is a spectacular and exciting sport, practised by over 17 million people in 70 countries worldwide. All you need is a surf-board and some waves. There are international surfing competitions, though most surfers see their sport more as a way of life. Many surfers are beach-lovers, who enjoy the excitement of coming into contact with the forces of nature. Some travel all over the world on a quest for the ultimate wave. Surfing has given rise to other sports – skateboarding, snowboarding, and windsurfing. All these sports offer adventure, challenge, and excitement.

Water polo

This Olympic sport was originally played in rivers and harbours, but is now played in swimming pools with a ball similar to that used in soccer. The modern game, with seven players per team along with a number of substitutes, requires considerable swimming skill. Water polo players need to be able to swim fast for short bursts, as well as have the endurance to last for four seven-minute quarters. In addition, they need to be able to catch and throw on the move. Standing on the bottom, or holding the side of the pool, is not allowed.

Getting to grips with the dynamic world of windsurfing.

Water-skiing

This exhilarating sport was invented in the US in 1922. Initially, it was an exhibition sport, but people started taking it up in large numbers as a hobby, and then competitively. There has been a World Championships event held once every two years since 1949. The three disciplines of water-skiing competitions are Figures, Slalom, and Jump. Water-skiers are awarded points for difficulty, style, and speed.

Professionals in competitions wear a swimming costume and a number. Others should wear a buoyancy aid and wetsuit.

Windsurfing

This sport combines aspects of both surfing and sailing and can be practised anywhere there is wind and water, by individuals of all ages and athletic abilities. The sail is attached to a mast and the windsurf board, and is manoeuvred to catch the wind and speed you along. Balance and an understanding of the wind are advantageous, but anyone can learn. No matter how good you are, there is always a new skill to learn. This is one of the reasons windsurfing is so addictive!

Water safety

LEARNING TO SWIM is the single best way to make yourself safe around water. However, swimming in a heated indoor swimming pool is very different from swimming outside. Over 80% of all drownings occur outdoors, in rivers, lakes, disused quarries, ponds, reservoirs, and the sea. It is therefore important that you know some water safety and rescue skills. A simple code, with four golden rules, will help you develop some lifeguarding sense. Remember it, and when you are out and about, your knowledge may help you become a real life-saver.

1 Take advice

Listen to the weather forecast before setting off for a swim. It may be warm and sunny inland but when you get to the coast the weather can be different or change suddenly. One of the biggest dangers to swimmers is the cold. Make sure you don't stay in the water too long and have a towel and warm clothes handy for when you get out. Always follow the advice of lifeguards, read all signs, and learn to recognise the flags shown here.

A chequered flag means surfboards only.

A red flag means don't swim.

A red over yellow flag means there is a lifeguard on duty.

On the beach

This beach is a good place to swim. The flag means there is a lifeguard on duty, and the black and white sign shows where it is safe to swim. Enjoy the beach but take care.

2 Check for dangers

Before you make a dash for the water, make sure you've checked that the place you've chosen to swim in is safe. Don't jump into very shallow water, imagining it to be deep. And don't go out of your depth if you're not a strong swimmer. The depth of water can be very deceptive.

A busy harbour

This picture shows an example of where NOT to swim. There is no lifeguard, the water may have strong currents, and be very cold and deep, and there are lots of boats milling around. It is dangerous to swim near boats, or off boats. You could be in danger of being hit by one, and they create currents in their wake that can pull you under.

Littering

Sharp rocks, tin cans, and glass in the water can cut your feet, so wear shoes to protect them. And don't leave any litter behind...

3 Don't swim alone

No-one should ever swim alone – not even lifeguards! Swim with your friends and family, and you'll have lots of fun. Always make sure someone knows where you are going, and when you'll be back.

4 Know how to help

It is important that you know what to do in the event of an emergency. If you see someone in trouble, stay calm and get help as quickly as you can.

Shout!

Shout loudly, not only to attract the attention of people near-by, but also try and guide the person in trouble to safety with clear instructions.

Throw a rope or something which floats – a ball, plastic bottle, or life buoy.

⚡ Emergencies

Try to help from the shore or land. Never put yourself at risk.

How to make an emergency float

Practise making a float from a pair of lightweight trousers. This skill will not only improve your water confidence, it could also help you cope in an emergency.

1 While treading water, soak the trousers in the water and tie a knot in the end of each trouser-leg.

Practise this exercise in your local pool.

2 Hold the trousers out by the waistband. Take a breath and pass the trousers behind your head. You may bob under the water, so keep holding your breath. Kick hard with your legs to keep afloat.

3 Keep hold of the waistband in both hands. Throw the trousers up and over your head to catch as much air as possible in the legs. Repeat until the trouser-legs are full of air.

4 Hold the waistband closed together and pull it just below the surface of the water. Rest your chin on your hands and let the float hold you up. Lie in the water and try to keep as still as possible.

Reaching out

Reach out with a stick, scarf, jumper, or anything long, but make sure you are secure. The girl in this picture is practising life-saving techniques in her local pool. She has thrown out a float to pull someone in and has secured herself by lying down.

Lifejacket

A lifejacket is essential if you are taking part in some water sports. It will keep you afloat and upright, with your head out of the water, if you accidentally fall in. You should wear a lifejacket even if you are a strong swimmer.

Glossary

During swimming practice, or when watching swimming events, you may find it helpful to understand the meaning of some of the following words and terms:

Sculling

A

Action Any movement of the limbs in swimming. For every action you perform there is an equal and opposite reaction.
Alternating strokes A term used to describe the crawl strokes.

B

Back crawl start A start for backstroke races. It begins in the water and is similar to a backwards dive.
Ballet leg A movement in synchronized swimming when one leg is lifted straight out of the water vertically, leaving the other leg horizontal at the water surface.

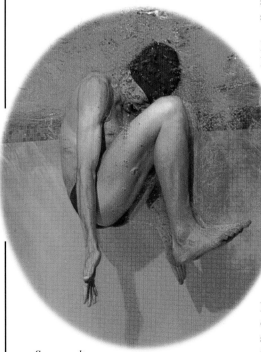

Somersault

Body roll A movement of the body towards the entering arm in front and back crawl.

C

Catch point The point at which the hand starts to exert pressure on the water. This occurs soon after the hand enters the water.
Competition pool A pool used for competitions, usually 50 m (164 ft) long. Sometimes there are movable booms and pool floors, so the length and depth can be adjusted.

D

Dive ring A weighted ring that is thrown into the pool to be picked up. It is used to practise swimming underwater with your eyes open.
Diving pit A diving pool, where the minimum depth is 3.5 or 5 m (11 or 16 ft), depending on the diving board heights.
Dolphin chain A formation in synchronized swimming where two back-to-back swimmers hold each other's feet, arch outwards, and rotate.
Dolphin kick An up-and-down kick used in butterfly when both legs kick together.
Drag Resistance in the water. A loose swimsuit may cause drag in the water and slow you down.

E

Entry point The point where a part of your body first breaks the surface of the water.
Explosive breathing A breathing technique where air is blown out quickly and forcefully before a new breath is taken.

F

False-start rope A rope used to stop swimmers if the starter decides that a race has started without his or her consent.
Figures A series of movements to make shapes with your body in synchronized swimming.
Finals The final race of an event that decides the overall winner. The fastest swimmers from the heats (see heat) go forward to the final.
Freestyle relay A swimming race where four **swimmers** each swim a leg, or section, using any **stroke**.
Front paddle A very basic swimming stroke that uses an alternating crawl-style leg kick and a paddling arm action. Also known as "doggie paddle".

G

Glide position A streamlined body position where the arms are outstretched close to the head. A glide can be performed on the water's surface or below it, and on the front or back.

H

Grab start The most common start in freestyle, breaststroke, and butterfly races. The competitor bends over and presses his or her hands against the starting block to begin the start.

Hand mitt A mitt made out of flexible material, that fits on to your hand and enables you to change your hand shape in the water; useful for arm-strengthening work.
Hand paddle A board that fits on to your hand and enables you to change your hand shape in the water; useful for arm-strengthening work.
Heat A race within an event. When there are more competitors than lanes in a pool, the competitors are divided into groups, or heats. Each group swims a heat and the swimmers with the fastest times go through to the finals.
High-lift style A style of breaststroke used by many swimmers to increase their speed.
Horizontal float A floating position when the swimmer's legs are together and arms by the side.

I

Intoeing A position of the feet, when they are turned inwards to give greater foot extension and make the foot a more effective paddle.

Surface dive

K

Kickboard Another name for a float. It is usually held in the hands when practising leg actions.

L

Lane marker A rope or wire, often with plastic discs on it, that runs the length of the pool and is used to stop people from swimming into each other's path.

Leg One complete section of a relay race. For example, in a 4 x 100 m relay, the four team members will each swim 100 m, or one leg, of the race.

Leisure pool A swimming pool specially designed for leisure activities.

Log roll A movement when a swimmer rotates, whilst horizontal in the water, with fully extended body, arms above the head, legs together.

M

Medley, Individual An event where competitors perform the following strokes over a set distance: butterfly, backstroke, breaststroke, and freestyle. The freestyle stroke cannot be one of the other three strokes.

Medley, Relay An event where teams compete against each other. Each team member swims a different stroke in the following order: backstroke, breaststroke, butterfly, and freestyle. The freestyle stroke cannot be one of the strokes already swum.

Mushroom float A float position when the swimmer is face down, with the body in a tucked position, and legs hugged to the body.

O

Oyster A figure of synchronized swimming when the swimmer submerges from a flat position on the surface by dropping the body down, with legs and hands towards the surface. The hands hold on to the ankles.

P

Pike A position adopted during the flight of some dives, when the swimmer's body momentarily bends at the hips.

Prone A swimming position where the swimmer lies on his or her front.

Propulsion Movement through the water as a result of leg or arm action.

Pull buoy A type of float that fits around a part of the body, enabling a swimmer to concentrate on another part. For example, pull buoys that fit on your legs help you to work on your arm techniques.

Push and glide position A position where the swimmer's body is fully extended so it is as streamlined as possible. It is used when pushing off from the poolside and gliding through the water.

R

Recovery The stage in a stroke sequence when the swimmer's legs or arms have finished the propulsive stage and are returning to their starting positions.

S

"S" pull An efficient backstroke arm action. The arm makes the shape of an "S" in the water. Also known as the bent arm action.

Screw kick An uneven leg kick used in breaststroke.

Sculling Propelling yourself through the water by moving your hands in small figure-of-eight movements.

Simultaneous strokes A term used to describe breaststroke and butterfly.

Star float A floating position where the swimmer stretches out on the surface of the water in the shape of a star.

Starting block A block on which swimmers stand to start a race. The block is attached to the poolside and has a non-slip surface.

Supine A swimming position where the swimmer lies on his or her back.

Surface dive A dive from the surface of the water, so that the swimmer is submerged.

T

Touch turn A racing turn used when swimming breaststroke and butterfly.

Track start A method of starting a race. The competitor gets into a position with one foot forward and one foot back and grips the starting block with his or her hands and toes. This start gives a big push-off.

Transition The period of time that you are under the water during a start or turn.

Treading water A way of staying afloat in the water. The legs usually perform vertical breaststroke and the arms scull close to the surface.

Trickle breathing A breathing technique where air is released gradually before a new breath is taken.

Tub A shape in synchronized swimming when the swimmer performs turning movements by using the hands whilst holding a position with his or her head; shins and feet are on the surface and the hips are dropped down.

Tumble turn A racing turn used in front crawl.

W

Wind-up start A start used in relay takeovers, where you build up momentum by circling your arms.

Floats

Goggles

Star float

Index

Useful addresses

Here are the addresses of some swimming organizations, which you may find useful.

The Amateur Swimming Association (ASA)
Harold Fern House
Derby Square
Loughborough LE11 5AL
England   Tel: 01509 618700

Welsh Amateur Swimming Association (WASA)
Roath Park House
Ninian Road
Cardiff
CF2 5ER   Tel: 01222 488820

The Scottish Amateur Swimming Association (SASA)
Holm Hills Farm
Greenlees Road
Camburslang
Glasgow G72 8DT
Scotland   Tel: 0141 641 8818

Swim Ireland
House of Sport
Long Mile Road
Dublin 12
Ireland   Tel: 00 3531 4568698

The Royal Life Saving Society
River House
High Street
Broom
Warwickshire
B50 4HN
England   Tel: 01789 773994

World Swimming Ruling Body:
Fédération Internationale de Natation Amateur (FINA)
Avenue de Beaumont 9
1012 Lausanne
Switzerland

Marvin Harry Lisa Greta Melanie Laura Kaya Jun Annabelle

Acknowledgements

Dorling Kindersley would like to thank the following people for their help in the production of this book:

With special thanks to: all the young swimmers for their skill, enthusiasm, and hard work; the swimmers' families; Alison Bell for advice on synchronized swimming; Putney Leisure Centre; Brigid Land and Andrew Jackson for assistance on the photo sessions; Hilary Gough (Swimming Development Officer at Wandsworth); Alan Guy and all the staff and children at Leander Swimming Club; Clare Brooker for lifeguard duties; Jenny Forest for the use of her pool; The Royal Life Saving Society UK for the use of their photos and valuable advice; the RYA–Windsurfing; British Water-ski; British Surfing Association; Noltan St Louis; Lesley Betts, Susan St Louis, Sophia Tampakopoulos, Claire Tindell for

design assistance; Patricia Grogan, Sarah Johnston, Stella Love for editorial assistance; Giles Powell-Smith for the jacket design.

Picture credits
key: b=bottom; l=left; r=right; c=centre; t=top; a=above; b=below
Action Plus/Neale Haynes: 15br; /Mike Hewitt: 28cr; /Glyn Kirk: 36cr; /DPPI: 36b; /Peter Tarry: 39cl; All Action/Al Bello: 37tr; Allsport/Al Bello: 10tl, 10tr; /Shaun Botterill: 28bl, 39tl; /Simon Bruty: 14-15, 25tr, 27tr, 29br, 31cr; /Michael Cooper: 14bl; /Mike Hewitt: 22cl; /David Leach: 14t; /Graham Bool: 37cl; /Bob Martin: 36cl; /Markus Boesch: 38br; Christel Clear Marine

Photography/ Christel Clear: 40tr; Colorific: Robert Garvey: 40bl; Colorsport: 11bl, 38tr; /Andrew Cowie: 15bl, 37bl; Mary Evans Picture Library: 11cra; Werner Forman Archive/The British Museum, London: 11t; Dan Helms: 10cl, 10bc, 24cla; The Image Bank/Gianalberto Cigolini: 35clb; Popperfoto: 11cla; The Royal Life Saving Society: 41tl, 41bl; US Swimming/Charlie Snyder: 10cr; Speedo: 11br; Sporting Pictures (UK) Ltd: 32tr, 36tr; /John Carter: 39br; Telegraph Colour Library: 26bl, 40br, 38cl; Topham: 11bc; Alan Towse Photography: 37tl; John Walmsley: 12bl. Back jacket: Tony Duffy. Endpapers: Action Plus/Mike Hewitt.